Business Fables

Robert Right

This book is dedicated to my wife.
God bless her for putting up with me through all of this stuff.

Contents

Boy, what I have learned in business! The hard way. Unfortunately, business school didn't teach me any of this stuff. It doesn't matter where you get an MBA, whether it's Harvard or online, or whether you even have an MBA or not. The real world of work is incredibly messy. Sadly, there are bad actors out there as well looking for smaller companies to take advantage of so that they make a fee, and the company gets nothing. I wrote this book as a wakeup call to those aspiring CFO's, so that they understand the risks involved in this career path (moving from a Fortune 500 into smaller companies so that you can move up). I also wrote this book for small business owners and the general public, so that they know what is really going on in the world of business today and watch out for these things. The best thing for anyone to do today is keep their sense of humor about all the things that will happen to them in their career. Only a very few seem to have a charmed path.

This book is a chronicle of my experience as a small and mid-size company CFO in America today. All of the stories actually happened. I was directly involved in most of these events. If not, then the events were relayed to me by the principals involved and occurred either before I started at a company or after I left. This book won't just be business facts. It will relay the emotional trauma that comes with it.

The world of work has changed tremendously since I started my career. There is far more competition for positions in the world of finance today than there was in the 1990's. If you look on LinkedIn, you will literally see thousands of unemployed former CFO's looking for work, especially those older than 50. Also, the demands of work and pace of work are far greater than they were thirty years ago. Work doesn't stop today. I have gotten text messages at 11:00 p.m. from business associates saying "why in the f*** aren't you answering your phone"? Suffice it to say, this kind of thing simply didn't occur back then. The world was far more genteel. Companies and senior management used to care about their employees as human beings and feel a sense of responsibility to the employee and their families. That compassion and empathy is exceedingly rare today (although as I finish this book, I am helping a family-owned business that still lives and breathes the old values that were once taken for granted).

Still, most of us continue to want the same things from work – good people to work with, an inspiring CEO and mission, and the opportunity to really contribute to our company. Here's wishing all of you these things and more as you commit the majority of your hours alive to "work", whatever that is for you.

Chapter 1
Don't Drink and Drive

John came to the company as CEO about six months after I had also joined Upcoming Software (not the real name of course) as CFO. John was a Fortune 100 senior sales executive in technology and knew the software industry well. I was excited! Finally, the company was going to have some real sales competency. Sales was the major area where the company just didn't seem to perform. The software was great but had not gained traction in the marketplace. People would do the demo and say they loved it, but still just not buy. John's arrival made me feel very hopeful, as I was considering leaving the company at the time and was in the interview process.

At first, John went to a lot of potential customer meetings with our Chairman Ted. They would always come back with big stories about how well the meetings were going and that we would "have a big, new client soon" that would change the company. Since I was never at these meetings, I had no way to know if the meetings were going well or not. Time went by with a lot of meetings, but I didn't see any new customer contracts that were signed (which I would have prepared), so I began to wonder what was really going on. I had always known that Ted exaggerated a lot, but John was too new to know if what he said was true or not. John repeatedly reassured me that a large client was imminent, and the new revenue would stabilize the company.

In the meantime, John started gradually coming in later and later, showing up at 10:00 or 10:30 after a while. Then he would go to lunch about 1:00, and I wouldn't see him in the office again. I figured this was good because a sales guy shouldn't be in the office. He should be out getting new business all day every day, right? But I found myself always asking Ron where John was and only got the answer "at a client's". As CFO, I needed John constantly to sign important documents or approve expenditures. I began to worry and honestly felt a little confused. What was going on with sales and still no new revenue?

After two to three months, I began to see e-mails from John to potential investors and investment bankers in the evening, sometimes late in the evening. I thought this guy has a serious work ethic! As a smaller company, we were always looking for new investment to continue our product launches. We simply would live or die based on whether we raised more money or not. However, eventually, the late-night e-mails started to have a different tone. They became confrontational with the bankers and potential investors, which is never a good thing. Bankers make big money and often have big egos. They are doing you the favor, not vice-versa. So, they really don't appreciate lip from the client. Fundraising takes a lot of time, and actual investors are rare. Patience is required. But John was quickly starting to lose patience with bankers critical to the business. He was alienating them. Now I was starting to get mad at John as well as worried.

We had been working with one investment banker named Richard for a few months. We had at least three in person meetings with Richard to go through due diligence (or financial statements and business plans) and work on our presentation materials. Later he brought two potential investors at two different times to hear the pitch from the company to get them to invest. Usually, one to two weeks would go by from the presentation prior to getting feedback on the meeting. When the meeting didn't go well, Richard usually would go "dark" for a while until he found another potential investor to whom we could give the pitch (he wouldn't answer his phone). Boy, did this make me mad.

You would think a banker would say "Joe took a pass, but I have x more presentations lined up" instead of just ignoring you. But Upcoming Software was desperate for money, so we basically had to put up with anything to stay alive. As the process dragged on though, my stress level was going up and up. Many nights I would wake up in the middle of the night with my heart racing. I wondered if I was going to have a heart attack. But Richard would reassure us when we were able to reach him. He would say that we were definitely going to succeed in raising new money.

Well, after a few months of this stuff with Richard, I was at home about 11:00 one night and happened to see an e-mail that had just gone out from John to Richard that was a classic, expletive laden tirade on Richard's capabilities (or lack thereof). I was thinking "holy shit, he just blew it!" Now we have very little cash and no investment banker. I went into the office the next day and asked Ted what was going on. Ted said, "Don't you get it yet? Not here in the mornings and afternoons and nasty e-mails after dinner? He's an alcoholic." "Oh shit", I said. My previous hope for the future of Upcoming Software vanished. Even worse, I had just passed up another good CFO role at a company with a functional CEO. That was when the Board started looking for a way to push John out, and I started trying to take most of the fundraising calls with bankers and prospects. What had seemed so promising when John first came on had turned into a disaster.

The lesson here is to be very, very careful in your hiring, especially for senior positions. The failure rate in senior recruiting is higher than it should be. Take a lot of time to really check your candidates out. An even better idea is to hire them on contract and make them permanent if their performance is as good as expected.

Chapter 2
Minnows and Whales

Bank Software was a startup with only $100,000 of revenue, and we were introducing a whole new technology to a staid industry. Progress launching our solution had been painfully slow. The need for new revenue was desperate. To speed up our maturation process, we decided to buy a much bigger company in the industry and use our technology on Acquiree's inventory to "prove that our software worked". We would then be able to show prospective clients concrete results of using our software. In theory, this idea was great. The reality turned out to be different and super stressful.

Acquiree was a leader in one of our prospective markets. It had over $60 million in revenue. This was a "minnow swallowing the whale" transaction because we were very small and the target company was much bigger. Obviously, we had to raise a lot of money. We hired a west coast investment banking firm for the deal. Banker 1 was a nationally known 2nd tier firm that would raise the $65 million we needed through a convertible debt structure. This means that the money was initially borrowed as a loan but could be converted to stock by the investor if the company did well and the stock gained a lot of value. We went through due diligence (checking out our financials and legal status), put the pitch book together that would show off the company and outline the deal terms for the potential investors, drafted all the acquisition agreements, stock documents, employment contracts, etc. The date to go out on the road show to try to get investors was approaching. Suddenly, Banker 1 wanted to change the deal structure to make it much more dilutive, meaning issuing much more stock. Instead of offering the conversion at $3.00 a share, Banker 1 wanted to offer the investors conversion at $1.25 per share. So, a $1,000 investment would convert to 800 shares rather than 334 shares. We said "no"! (In retrospect, we should have said "yes". At that moment, it didn't matter what the conversion price was. The deal would have been done, and we would have moved on.) But instead, we had to find a new investment banker.

Very luckily, the new banker that we found was top drawer from a 1st tier firm. Also, Banker 2 was from a technology investment bank, which made a lot more sense for our deal type as a software company buying a traditional business. We were super excited. Banker 2 and her team went back through due diligence again with us. They were a lot more thorough than the first firm, which was a good sign. We had to completely change our business plan for the type of investors we were now going to approach. Once again, we got the pitch book for potential investors put together to show off the company and the deal terms and went out on the road to speak with them. This time, we changed the deal structure on Banker 2's advice to a three-part structure with one layer of equity, one of layer of mezzanine debt (unsecured debt sitting between the equity and senior debt at a higher interest rate) and one layer of senior secured debt (like a bank loan) at a lower interest rate. We started working on the senior debt first as it was the easiest to place, since the investor would be fully secured by collateral of our assets. It is very exciting to be working on a deal with a top investment bank. Every day was a challenge and a thrill.

We talked to a lot of potential lenders, and I ended up going by myself to one lender that we thought was a low chance of being interested. I was a little nervous but excited to be going out on my own. It turned out that they liked our deal and agreed to place the senior debt. They also gave us a good contact for the mezzanine debt, and within thirty days we had that piece committed as well. The hardest layer to place was the equity piece since we had almost immaterial revenue but were buying substantial revenue. Equity investors invest usually betting that the stock price will go up, which is a speculative return. We went to firm after firm, from the big boys (private equity and venture shops) to the specialty equity guys. It was amazing how many potential investors our investment banker knew. We were nearing the end of our list. Finally, just before we were about to run out of potential equity sources, we ended up at a shop that liked our deal and gave us an offer letter to invest. We went out to celebrate! It would be hard to overstate how excited we all were after almost a year of working on the deal. Again, documents were drafted and prepared for a closing where the money would be funded, the acquisition would be completed and the target company's revenue would be ours.

One day out of the blue as closing was approaching, we got a call from the private equity firm selling Acquiree. They were getting on a plane and coming to see us in person at 10:00 a.m. the next morning. This sudden meeting couldn't possibly be good news, and it wasn't. With only a few weeks left until the close, the seller told us that the CEO of Acquiree had been committing fraud by cooking the books. He was falsely inflating the revenue to make sure that the deal would go through and had been immediately fired. We told the PE seller that the purchase price had to be significantly adjusted downward to reflect the actual revenue and operating profit of the target company. They agreed to drop the price from $65 million to $54 million, which was quite a concession. We had to redo all the deal documents and go back to each of the potential lenders and investors. Surprisingly, they agreed to still do the deal at the lower price *provided* there was no further falloff in revenue and profit. I was stressed beyond belief at this point. I wondered how I dealt with it and kept going, but I did. Every day I wondered if the purchase would be completed.

By this point, there was about two more weeks to the closing. The closing date was scheduled, and all the documents were revised and prepared for execution. Wire instructions were given for the funding of the purchase price and working capital at the closing. The final checkpoint was two days before the closing when the target company had to report revenue and operating profit to the group. Every day the interim CEO of the target assured us that everything was on track for the month and that the deal would close. He even said so the day before reporting would happen. The end-of-month reporting date came. I was very nervous. I had a bad feeling. Late that evening, the call went out. Not only had Acquiree missed the revenue number. They had missed badly with revenue off by another 40%. The deal was dead. Ten months of very hard work went down the drain in a flash. We were left with no money and huge expenses run up during the acquisition process and trying to figure out a way forward. It was a restart. I was very upset and disappointed. I didn't know how the company would survive with terrible financial statements because of all the expenses. As it turned out, the company didn't make it as it was running and effectively closed down for a year before restarting.

The lesson here is to be very, very careful in doing acquisitions. Make sure that the company is sound, but most importantly make sure that the existing management of the company you are considering buying is honest and not hustlers. If the CEO of the target comes off to you as a fast talker or hustler, move on to another potential company to buy.

Chapter 3
Spend Like a Drunken Sailor

It is amazing how quickly a company can go through money, especially when it has modest to no revenue yet. SpendIt was founded by acquiring a public shell (non-operating company). The shell had been in existence for several years and was publicly reporting during that period, meaning that financial statements had been published even though the company had almost no activity. When SpendIt acquired the shell, reporting continued, which would allow the company to trade on a real stock exchange once all the requirements were met. That process takes a lot of time and a lot of money. Often, it can be worth the effort because finding private money for a startup is more difficult. Once you are public, you can raise money more easily if you have a real business plan, because there are a lot of people who trade in the stocks of very small companies.

The legal bills alone to qualify to trade on a stock exchange are astounding. The money raise being done was mid-seven figures. Legal bills to achieve public trading easily run to half a million dollars. There are very lengthy, complicated documents that must be drafted and filed with the U.S. Securities and Exchange Commission in order to trade on an exchange. These documents tell all about the company's business, who its competitors are, what the risk factors of the investment are, and of course complete historical financial statements for 2-3 years to show the investor how the company is doing. The officers have to certify the financial statements and have personal financial liability for their accuracy. It's a big deal for the officers.

Then there is also about a quarter million of fees to the auditors for all the required financial due diligence and specialized financial reporting required for the public offering. The auditors have to perform a super audit to verify all of the numbers that are being put into the public offering documents as accurate, as auditors also have special liability to the public in these kinds of fundraising activities. So, the auditors are very picky and demanding about seeing all of the backup for all of the numbers in the financial statements and make many changes to their format.

Also, there are significant fees from the public relations people to promote the company so that the offering will be successful. The PR firm has to put together what are called "white papers" that talk about the company, its products and services and its potential in the future. The PR firm also prepares numerous press releases to talk about the current activities of the company or about new officers of the company. The PR firm is highly coordinated with the investment bankers.

Finally, and largest of course, are the fees paid to the investment bankers out of the money raised, but those fees are well earned if the offering is successful. Investment bankers are paid for their relationships with people who will put substantial money into new or existing companies. They make large fees because raising money is very difficult for most companies unless they are very large and well established. For newer companies, they are the gatekeepers to success. Most investment banks get paid 6% of the money that they raise for equity and 2% for debt. Debt is usually secured and safer, so that is why the fees are smaller. Equity is higher risk and much higher potential reward if the stock price really goes up.

SpendIt went out on the road show to try to get investors. The presentation was done in L.A., San Francisco, Chicago, Dallas, Atlanta and of course New York. The software that had been developed and patented was far ahead of its time at the point of the offering, so it was well received. Surprisingly, no one objected to the fact that there were no well-known sales executives affiliated with SpendIt at the time of the raise, a critical weakness. That problem was still to be addressed.

The offering was successful, and trading began on the exchange. After all the fees and expenses were paid, SpendIt received about half of the gross total raised, as there was also previous minor debt to be repaid. The bridge debt was incurred prior to the public offering to keep the company alive and pay bills during the six-month (that became nine-month) preparation period for public trading. The offering resulted in several million dollars, free and clear. Not an insignificant sum, or so it seemed at that moment.

Then came the business dinners and travel all over the place trying to get customers. Fancy restaurants for prospective clients with checks of several thousand dollars, trade shows at about twenty thousand each, a holiday party, trips to Las Vegas, California and a lot more. The company was burning over $250,000 of cash every month. All legitimate for a big company with a lot of revenue. Really pushing it for a small company with almost no revenue and trying to get revenue. It is shocking (and maddening) how many companies spend a fortune on marketing activities and never measure the results of those activities to see which ones are leading to sales and which are wasted money that do not increase sales.

Added onto all these travel and entertainment expenses was an ill-conceived ancillary business startup with the wrong people picked to run it. The industry "experts" hired predicted substantial profits when losses actually happened. Even worse was small acquisition with heavy ongoing losses that further drained the company's cash. This acquisition was burning more than $100,000 a month as well. To say that all this activity was poorly planned would be the understatement of the century. For my part, at least all this stupidity occurred prior to my arrival.

Long story short, I start work at the company five months after the offering and arrived to find the till almost empty. (The public statements showed a huge cash balance that had been drained in the following three months.) How could this happen?

The lesson of the story is that it happens by running a startup like a big company, with big company sales and marketing plans, big company expense allowances, big company salaries and all big company executives. There are tremendous differences between large corporations and small/startup businesses. Many executives who transition from one to the other simply don't understand that much of what works at a Fortune 500 doesn't work in a startup! Every expense must be questioned. Any expense that can be put off must be put off. Tradeoffs must be made because there is not enough money to do everything at once. However, the biggest failure was thrashing around trying several different things to create revenue (the core business, the ancillary business and the small acquisition) with no expertise in any of them, all while taking away resources and time from the original core business, causing it to flounder instead of takeoff. Also, picking all the wrong people to run these businesses was fatal in itself. Finally, for a CFO, the stress of a situation like this one is unbelievable, and that stress leads to a lot of anger that can carry over into other areas of life, unfortunately. For me, this was the end of working for startups with no revenue. The risk is too high unless you are already independently wealthy.

Chapter 4
I Don't Understand What "Startup" Means

Sad to say, there are companies that raise money to employ former big company executives who may not have developed achievable business plans yet. I have seen this problem more than once. That doesn't necessarily mean that the executives have bad intentions. It just means that they take care of themselves first in the name of running the business. The thinking goes that "the business will never get anywhere without me, and I have a family to feed and send to college". All of that may be true, but this approach is not one typically used by startups that are successful. The ones that succeed often involve significant upfront financial sacrifice by the founders so as not to drain the new company of all its capital. This self-sacrifice is not the mentality of former big company executives.

One example of the problem is the story of what I will call Newtech. Newtech had two founders, Paul and Johnny. It was started in a very wealthy area with access to a lot of capital from exceptionally successful people. Newtech also had a strong advantage in that Johnny knew an awful lot of people in this area because of his "day job". Johnny's education was technical, and Newtech was being created to launch a new energy technology. The concept was promising and had the potential to solve a couple of big problems for humanity. Patents had been filed. So, it attracted a lot of initial interest that led to a decent first round of investment of a few hundred thousand dollars.

The challenge was the other founder Paul, who was devoting all his time to launch the company. Paul was used to big salaries and big expense accounts. The technology came from a foreign country, which led to expensive trips to that country to develop the business plan and verify the validity of the technology. The technology had been proven in parts on different applications but had not been proven as a beginning-to-end system for its new application in energy. It was easy to get people to see the potential but hard to develop enough engineering detail to "prove" that it would work and therefore protect investors.

Besides the big cost of launching the project including the travel, the technology was expensive to build and therefore required substantial subsidies to generate the kind of return that would be required to fund a couple of hundred-million-dollar project. Only certain countries (not the U.S.) provided those subsidies, so it was decided that the first project would be in Europe, where subsidies were provided to get the project financed. The subsidies were credits which made the cost of this new energy comparable to traditional technology to make electricity. So, lots of trips to Europe suddenly became necessary to find the project site, go through due diligence with financers and get the project financed. A process like that is very expensive, so more money had to be raised. A couple of hundred thousand more was secured, but meanwhile, the founder's high salary of a quarter of a million and thousands of travel expenses continued to rack up.

Tens of thousands of dollars that was needed to pay the engineers, a deposit for the site of $100,000, the construction people in the tens of thousands and various consultants and lawyers essential to the success of any project instead went to pay executive salaries. Vendor bills got further and further behind. In addition, Paul and Johnny decided to build a large project as the first project, when some of the employees (principally me) advocated for a much smaller, more affordable demonstration project to prove the technology and show the returns that would actually accrue to the investors. Since it was a brand-new configuration of technologies, it was essential to show that a project would work as designed and provide the comfort necessary to investors to fund multiple additional projects so the technology could be rolled out repeatedly. This aspect was especially important because the company typically makes very little if any profit on the first project until everyone knows it works, and then the repeat business can be very profitable for the company.

Ultimately, the "farm" was bet on this one-track solution of the big project because of the ego of Paul. Paul liked to go for the home run, not the single to get to first base and then score later. Because the more expensive project was chosen and because of the ongoing drain of resources to big executive salaries, the company closed due to these bad decisions on project and pay. The big project was never developed, while another company with a different philosophy and technology built a small project on the original demonstration site that was rejected by Newtech. That competitive project was completed and became successful, thereby demonstrating its technology and securing additional funding for further projects.

The lesson is that bigger is definitely not always better, and if you are going to launch a startup you better be ready to make the necessary sacrifice. If you don't have enough personal resources to do without, don't start the startup! Also, with new technologies, do a smaller project to demonstrate the viability of the technology before building the huge project. A smaller project makes it easier to raise the money by lowering the amount needed and by decreasing the investor's initial risk.

Chapter 5
Optimistic and Then Some

Optimism is an important and valuable characteristic of leaders. This characteristic is important to business as well. The true visionaries in business have a view of a future fundamentally changed for the better in some respect because of their activities. However, unbridled optimism in business can lead to disaster.

Renewal was a company in a multi-billion-dollar industry with big and small players. Its position was fair – it was one of the bigger small companies by revenue and had profitable months and losing months. Profitability was principally determined by monthly volume in this business of relatively narrow margins. So, sales were everything, and the company was principally dependent on one major customer to determine its monthly fortunes. Many companies in the $5-10 million revenue range fit this exact description. They have enough revenue to be stable and marginally profitable but not enough to really break out and expand. The dependence on a single large customer also entails significant risk, because if that customer decides to reduce its purchases by say 30-50% one day, you are out of business.

Renewal had a large investment in it by a private equity fund, Fund It, which had made the investment based on the industry expertise of the young entrepreneur who had founded it. Fund It believed that Renewal had reached the size that it needed professional management in addition to the Founder. The Founder agreed. Not all founders agree to this kind of change because they enjoy total control and don't want to give any of it up. Renewal's Founder was unusual in that he was open to learning from anyone.

The new company president, Martin, brought in by Fund It, was brilliant and very optimistic. Martin initiated many great changes, including diversifying the company's product mix and customer base to reduce the reliance on the very large customer. These changes were prudent strategy. However, Martin had to commute from across the country, so he started thinking about how to move the company across the country closer to his home. Two of the primary justifications developed were that Renewal needed a more modern facility with a proper layout to get more of the kind of new customers that it really needed and to increase production efficiency, and that the employee base was better in the new location with more qualified people available as the company grew.

There was one problem. Renewal was extremely tight on cash flow. It was so tight that making payroll was the priority, while other general bills often became significantly extended. This situation is very stressful for a CFO as vendors constantly call looking for payment. With at least three small companies that I have been with, vendors only held off legal action based on my rapport with them and effort to give them something as often as I could. Moves are also very expensive. The cost of preparing the new space, moving the inventory and getting needed equipment for a much bigger space would cost $2 million, a significant portion of the company's revenue (much less its limited profit). Objections were raised, but Martin prevailed with the Founder, the board and Fund It, and the move was on. The Taj Mahal was built. It truly was an impressive facility.

To pay for the move which would cost about $200,000, this money was borrowed very short term to get the company through the actual move. A significant portion of the short-term loans were committed to rapid repayment. A separate bridge loan (which is a loan between the short-term funding and long term permanent financing) was arranged after the short-term funding that was intended to keep the company open through the first six months' after the move while revenue ramped up again. However, much of the bridge loan was committed to repaying the outstanding short term money borrowed during the move, leaving the company critically depleted of cash. In addition, due to the several months that it took to arrange the bridge loan (which would pay for the rest of the project), construction ended up being delayed by 90 days. Thus, the company was totally closed for 2-1/2 months before the new facility was ready, because a firm move out date had been established on the old facility. The original building had been sold. The company had to move out on July 31, but then due to funding delays the new building didn't open until mid-October. The company was therefore in a very difficult position. The delayed move and months closed stopped revenue completely while the money that had been borrowed all had to be repaid quickly.

After moving in, it became apparent that more cash was needed urgently. An emergency fundraising effort was begun. A new investment banker was hired. The whole fundraising process started over with new presentations, due diligence and business plans required. Hours and hours were spent on yet another raise. Potential investors were interested, but the raise failed because any potential new money required a substantial cram down of Fund It, the prior investor. They had to give up a significant percentage of their ownership, from roughly 67% down to about 30%, and be delayed in repayment of their loans until after the new investor had made its required return of 15%. Fund It balked, the potential investors walked, and the company ran out of cash and closed 5-1/2 months after the move.

The critical error though was structuring a move that required everything to go perfectly for Renewal to survive. The reality is that nothing ever does go perfectly in business (or life). Overly optimistic plans killed the company when not enough cash was raised, delays in fundraising and therefore construction occurred, and more time was needed to turn around a balky substantial prior investor.

For Fund It, the situation became a total disaster. Instead of ending up with a viable company but having to wait quite a while for a return on the investment, millions of dollars were lost forever by the investor. Instead of giving up half of their stock so that the company had enough new money come into the company for it to reach profitability, they lost millions of dollars of their investment. This loss hugely impacted their private equity fund. Their investors started demanding immediate withdrawal of their money and repayment for their losses. Fund It had put so much money into Renewal that it didn't have the money to return to the investors or cover the losses. Fund It nearly went out of business itself.

The lesson is that optimism must be tempered with backup planning for the worst-case scenario. Clear, achievable planning must be in place for what to do when things inevitably go wrong. As the Wall Street guys say, "You have to protect the down side." In this case, there needed to be viable plans for delays in funding, delays in completion of construction and delays in revenue ramping back up or it taking longer than expected to get to profitability. If good, achievable plans had been in place to cover these contingencies, then Renewal would still be open, Fund It wouldn't have lost all its investment, and all of the employees wouldn't have been put out of work.

On a final note, this situation was the third in a row where I began to miss paychecks. From the CEO's, it was always the same. "Just hang in there, things will get better, you will get paid, and we will all retire in a few years." For those of you out there thinking about leaving a big company to move up in a smaller one, quit immediately when the paychecks start to be late.

Chapter 6
Build It and They Will Come

The second story of overly optimistic planning is legendary. It is the infamous "build it and they will come" mistake.

Negotiate was founded based on a brilliant idea. It was so brilliant that the method was patented back in 1998, the early days of method patents. Negotiate was the second company started using this method patent as applied to software, with each allowed to use the patent in different markets from each other. Some of the best available programming talent was bought in during the early 2000's to build this second application. The result was some software that everyone who saw it raved about. It was intuitive, consumer friendly, relatively simple to use on the administrative end and would integrate with any existing platform that potential customers were using, although about 30 days of implementation work was required (which is nothing if you know software implementations). Finally, the new software was tested in focus groups with very positive results. It was time to launch.

This new software was focused at a consumer facing industry with many very large players in one segment and a wide range of players from very small to fairly large in the other segment. Robert, the founder, was convinced based on initial feedback to the software that adoption would be quick. As you might guess, there were two cases of "however" that would arise. The first "however" was that Robert brought in a medium size staff, with most of the staff in IT (programming and hardware) and accounting, but never hired competent sales staff. Robert's view was that once someone saw the software demonstrated that it was so obviously beneficial to the business that anyone would use it. Wrong. Like all new products, the software needed a true and strong sales competency to make customers see the value in it. Sure, it was easy to use, but can you give me a clear value proposition? Can you show me that I will make double my investment in the software in additional profit? Because there were no good salespeople working for the company, the answer was "no", so pricing ended up being all over the place and was moving downward, and prospects started demanding "free trials" and then they would decide if they would sign up and pay for the software. For a startup with limited cash, free trials are a death march. Negotiate had to have revenue as quickly as possible. Even after a trial would take place, there was still no salesperson who could clearly state the value added (ROI – return on investment), quantify it and show it based on actual results to the potential customer. This was an epic marketing failure.

The second "however" was that the software was targeted at a very conservative industry. From day one of launching the software, it quickly became clear that adoption would be slow. For the first segment of mostly very large prospects, the sales cycle was 18-24 months. The sales cycle was this long because multiple demonstrations had to be scheduled for successive layers of management, then Negotiate might have to go through a formal bidding process, and then if Negotiate won the bid the company had to go through the Vendor Qualification group for a check of financial and legal status. For the second segment with a varied range of prospects, the sales cycle was 60 days at the small end of the client spectrum where you were dealing with individual decision makers and 12-18 months at the fairly large end of the client spectrum because the sales process was similar to the first segment of very large prospects. What did this mean for a startup? You can guess what it meant. At first, Robert went after segment one, because securing one client would constitute a "home run", instantly transforming the company from a startup to a mid-size player in the industry and profitability. It's always hardest to get the first client. Again, the industry was very conservative, so none of these very large players would take a risk on new technology. Their view was that it was unproven. They wanted to know that someone else had already used the software successfully. In addition to a poorly quantified value proposition, these very large businesses required their vendors to be credit worthy before they could work with them. As a startup, Negotiate was still cash flow negative and therefore not creditworthy.

After two years of futility and running out of cash several times, Negotiate was recapitalized with more outside money and refocused on the small end of the customer base in segment two with the 60-day sales cycle in order to build some revenue. While about ten clients were secured in this group of prospects, two problems remained. First and foremost, the company still couldn't clearly state and prove the value proposition even to these small clients because of not hiring a competent sales staff. Customers want to know dollars saved for dollars spent (ROI). Second, these small clients did not generate enough revenue to justify the implementation and support costs, much less to support the business and move it toward profitability. Ten clients at $1,000 per month for $10,000 of revenue doesn't really help when your expenses are still $50,000 per month. You just couldn't get enough revenue to be profitable unless you could get bigger clients with more volume, but those clients were the most risk averse.

They were much more difficult to get, even if you could have proven a strong return on the investment in the software. So, Negotiate and Robert built it, but they did not come. $40 million of investment over 10 years ended up being wasted and lost by the investors. To this day, Negotiate limps along with no real revenue from its software, although twelve years later it went into a different business that now generates some real revenue that continues to keep Negotiate alive.

The lesson is that "build it, and they will come" almost never works (except for the literal one in a million like Google).

Chapter 7
On Being All Things to All People

Business today is tough. Beyond tough, when now only a few businesses do not compete globally or with huge companies with far better funding. All the literature tells you that you must do everything possible to service or attract clients/customers. While taking care of the people who pay you is obviously critical, it can lead to a serious business mistake. I call this mistake "we can be all things to all people", which of course no company can be.

SoftIT grew up as a software company focused on one particular client base. In all small businesses, cash is king. To get sales, the company management instructed the sales people to start selling to anyone they could think of who might use the software. Within a short period, the company was trying to sell into at least five different types of clients. There are many problems with this approach.

First, small companies, as desperate as they may be for revenue, usually have limited (or very limited) resources. The biggest limiting factor is the number of people working there who can get each specific task done. So, it gets impractical very quickly to thoroughly research and understand more and more potential customer types, their needs and what would drive them to buy your product or service (i.e., proper marketing). Many small companies ignore these marketing activities completely and go straight to the sales process with little or no planning. Even if you can do the research and gain an adequate level of understanding of your markets and customer needs, then how do you translate that knowledge into actionable materials targeting these prospective client sectors? This step in the process is very time consuming. Worse, when not done well, you get no traction in that sector you are targeting because you are not clearly addressing your prospective clients' needs in a way that means something to them. I previously discussed how disastrous it is to not be able to clearly state and prove your value proposition to each customer type based on their specific needs.

Second, product innovation is critically important. But if you are small and targeting multiple sectors, whose needs get addressed first? How is a priority for enhancements set? Where does adequate capital come from to address the innovation needed for one sector much less three or five? Product innovation is best done in a focused way. There must be strong knowledge of one sector, a real understanding of customer needs in the sector, and the focus and discipline to deliver a differentiated product that clearly stands out against all the competition. These ingredients are the critical path to eventual sales success.

Third, you can't get enough people who really know what they are doing in so many different markets. It is quite hard today to attract truly qualified talent to adequately address one sector. Your business must have a strong reputation to attract top talent in a given field. This people problem is central to the success of any business. Some researchers believe that business success is driven first by picking the right team and then afterward addressing product and market issues. Successful business books have been written about the top performing companies and that they are so successful because they picked a brilliant team first and then outperformed their business sector on stock price.

The problem with this philosophy is that it only applies to well established companies that are trying to get better and not so much to new or smaller companies. Small companies usually can't attract top corporate executives.

However, most successful businesses today of any size do one thing and try to do it better than anyone else. Then you can become a magnet for your most important resource (people), providing you offer an employee centered environment (which most companies today sadly do not). Depth of expertise in one subject matter is a potent competitive weapon in any field that also insulates you from the normal ups and downs of any market. You become THE choice in the marketplace.

Finally, of course, is money, which impacts all the above but also has additional elements not already covered. Making payroll at all is often a challenge for smaller companies. Every entrepreneur that I have worked with views payroll as their most sacred duty and biggest challenge, as it comes every one or two weeks for most companies no matter what, and making it is often a struggle. Then there is cost of equipment, rent, utilities, office expenses, insurance, etc. It is simply impossible for a small business to effectively meet all these obligations and then to have the "extra" cash to address multiple markets/sectors. The lesson is that success with a scattergun approach is highly unlikely.

SoftIT has been in business for 13 years and still has no meaningful revenue. "Throw it against the wall and see what sticks" simply doesn't work. Small companies almost never have the resources to pursue multiple markets or products in their early stages. It is far better to pick one thing and do it better than anyone else.

Chapter 8
Desperation Leads to Bad Choices

The most desperate need of any small company is money. Having it is the only way to get any idea off the ground. For most new small businesses, the options for raising money to start are very limited. In the current environment, banks won't lend for a new business unless you are already so creditworthy that you don't need the money or simply want to use their cash instead of yours. Any bank lending comes with the requirement of personal guarantees, which is toxic if you aren't liquid for cash. You don't want to borrow for a new business against your home. Safety for family comes first. So, for most, banks are not an option.

Without banks, you must get creative. A lot of non-bank business lenders have sprung up since the 2008-2009 recession. The problem with these non-bank lenders is that they also want a personal guarantee on all your assets, so these types of sources are also a non-starter. You can go angel or venture, but often they want a very large percentage of your business for a small amount of initial investment. SaveIt went with another option. The founder, Bob, found a cheap public shell (again, a non-operating company reporting financials to the public, which are getting more and more hard to find) and then had a public vehicle with which to raise money. Even with the shell, you still don't want venture or private equity because you must give up a big percentage or outright control. So, Bob met and started working with a solo guy in California who raised money from wealthy people and/or family offices.

Tom was a character, to put it mildly. He had a very outgoing personality, was very smart, related well to people and knew a lot of super wealthy folks. On the surface, he was the perfect rainmaker for the company. SaveIt prepared all the investment materials and instructed Tom on what he could and couldn't say to potential investors. The trouble was that Tom was very results oriented and a bit of a free spirit. It quickly became apparent that when Tom was by himself with a prospect, very optimistic results for the investment were promised. SaveIt was constantly having to "fact check" and correct what the prospect was told when they were turned over to the company to secure the investment and do the documents. SaveIt's needs were dire, so it had to go with the flow when it came to Tom. Tom did produce amazing results. Tom raised a lot of money and earned significant finder's fees. Tom in particular had a knack of finding an investor at the last possible minute when the company was faced with immediate failure, therefore saving the day once again.

During a few of these critical periods, Tom would disappear. Usually, Tom was always available and very responsive to the company. However, every so often and correlated to payment of a large finder's fee, Tom would go off the grid. Phone calls weren't answered, voicemail filled up and SaveIt's management was left to wonder where he was and what was going on. Well, it didn't take more than six months to find out what was going on. Tom had been in and out of rehab, and with cash flush in his pocket, a binge would come on, usually involving Las Vegas. When the cash was gone, Tom would resurface and be available to the company again to raise more money. Tom was actually one of several people that I worked with in my career who had substance problems. This issue is more common in business that one would think. With the older guys, it's the booze and long lunches or not returning to the office after lunch. With the younger guys, it was more serious stuff or coming in hung over a lot and not being very productive in the morning. So, SaveIt found itself depending for its life on someone brilliant but unpredictable and with issues. My bet is that a lot of executives have experienced this phenomenon.

The lesson here is that you have to be very careful who you get into business with out of desperation. When you are down, it is very easy to get involved with the wrong people or make a mistake that results in your original problems becoming much worse.

Chapter 9
The Bullshit Artist

Startup was constantly in fundraising mode. It had worked with a lot of different types of lending sources but tended toward the unconventional because it was not eligible for asset-based lending. At one point, Startup was introduced to a guy named Frank. Frank was presented as a big shot, a global financier based in the Upper Midwest who had interests around the globe and worked with some big name financial institutions anyone would know. References were requested and given. He seemed to check out.

Startup was public. So, management had to follow a set and strict process when dealing with this kind of investor. After the reference checks, the next step was to develop a preliminary deal structure acceptable to Frank and Startup. Tremendous work went into developing different scenarios internally that would give Frank substantial potential upside but not dramatically dilute the company. A preliminary valuation was established for discussion purposes, and a proposed structure was finally developed that included a board seat for Frank. He was going to bring "unbelievable resources" to bear post-investment that would launch the company on a new trajectory, not just because of the funding but also through all his top tier relationships.

Due diligence began. Reams of materials were sent to Frank's analyst almost daily. Each submission had to be reviewed during a follow up conference call. Days and days were spent on these conference calls. Each call resulted in new requests, more internal work and then the presentation of the new material to Frank and his analyst. After about six weeks of long days, Frank finally told the company that it had cleared due diligence for the investment. Since I was the primary liaison on the due diligence and spoke to Frank's analyst much of every day, it seemed that their group knew what it was doing. Frank used all the top tier investment banking firm practices and procedures.

Now came the very expensive part – deal documents and accounting certifications. Startup had always used a top New York law firm. That was how it had gone public. Frank used a top DC law firm as his counsel. The initial call with Frank, his analyst, his lawyers, Startup and its lawyers took place. Keep in mind that these firms typically bill about $500 per hour per person, and there was at least a three-person team engaged at each law firm (resulting in about $1,500 per hour billable). Then the back and forth, back and forth started between the two law firms. After about two weeks and over $100,000 of legal fees, the documents were finally agreed to between Frank and Startup and all the attorneys. There was also a $15,000 bill from the auditors for their certification that the financial statements were free of material errors. At this point, about ten weeks of time had been spent on the deal, which was not unreasonable for a very large financing.

The formal closing and celebratory lunch were scheduled. The big day came, and it was big for Startup, because it was the closing of a $15MM investment, the largest in company history by far. A board meeting was scheduled for the next week where Frank would formally join the board. Frank had his attorneys sign the documents because he was "closing another deal" that day. A public announcement of the investment was released to all the shareholders and media by Startup. Everyone went to lunch, and the wire was "initiated" (started). By late in the day, the wire had not arrived. Frank's attorneys from the top tier firm strongly emphasized that the wire was on the way and not to worry.

By the next day, the worry had set in. No wire. Frank said that he was converting cash from Europe that had to go through Hong Kong and therefore was delayed. The wire would be in by the next day. Well, the next day came, there was no wire, but Frank provided a letter from a Texas bank certifying that the wire was in route. What relief! Only the wire continued not to show up day after day. In the meantime, Startup was forced to put out weekly updates on the status of the wire because of the original press release. How embarrassing! Frank and his analyst were unreachable by this point. Call after call went unreturned. Embarrassment turned to rage.

Fast forward three months. One day, the FBI called making inquiries about Frank. They spent about two hours on the phone with us, as Frank was implicated in several frauds with other companies where he had taken money from them for specific services and then disappeared. Startup mentioned about the letter from the Texas bank confirming the wire. Well, the bank officer was fired and prosecuted. The bank settled with Startup for $500,000. What about the attorneys from the top tier firm in DC? The company sought the $15 million from the law firm. The firm fired the attorneys and made a nuisance value (small) payment to Startup. Without the investment, Startup was severely cash strapped after all the previously incurred legal and accounting fees and couldn't afford to litigate the fraud.

Such is life in the small, desperate company scratching for dollars to literally stay alive! The lesson here is that you must pick your battles carefully, as most of them you can't even fight, much less win. Don't waste resources that are needed for sales and marketing. The focus always has to be on the customer!

Chapter 10
You Don't Know What You Don't Know

The final story is a cautionary tale of acquisitions. BuyIt was a new company and needed revenue fast, as it had a large burn rate (negative cash flow). One of the ways to fix this problem if you have a bit of extra cash is to buy the revenue by acquisition and become instantly profitable. This idea certainly has the appeal of simplicity and perhaps speed (depending on the situation), but the execution of it is an entirely different challenge. Most smaller companies have very poor skills when it comes to acquisitions. They don't properly cast an adequately sized net for potential targets. They don't have the in-house skills for deal structure, negotiation and due diligence. Often, they don't even have the operational skills to run the new acquisition as they are still inexperienced and consumed with trying to get the parent company on its feet. This story highlights all those issues and more.

BuyIt had heard about BadCo being for sale on an urgent basis. BuyIt was located close to the sellers of BadCo, but the actual operations of BadCo were on the other side of the country. BadCo was for sale due to serious financial problems of its own. So, you had a startup with barely any revenue buying a business already in real trouble. The price was right. Relatively little cash was required to buy BadCo, as the sellers would take stock in BuyIt. From a deal structure perspective, the transaction was reasonably structured.

The wheels came off the bus when it came to the due diligence on BadCo. The CFO of BuyIt had scheduled a trip out of the country six months earlier and was therefore out of the country when the sellers contacted

BuyIt. The CEO of BuyIt, John, was not known for patience, so he went on with the transaction in the CFO's absence. Two supposedly very experienced industry experts were engaged to do the due diligence, and there were transaction files following the deal showing the due diligence done, but of course the result of the checking up on BadCo proved to be wholly inadequate. The CFO therefore returned from being away to find that an acquisition had been completed in her absence and without her input.

Well, that poor CFO returned to find out that the former BadCo and now new division of BuyIt was burning $800,000 of cash a month. This painful truth only added to BuyIt's problems in a big way. BuyIt was already burning $400,000 per month, for a new combined total monthly cash loss of $1.2 million. The new combined company certainly had meaningful revenue now on the order of $10 million annually, but it was burning a tremendous amount of cash. The CFO had already told management before her trip that she was going to leave BuyIt, so she had an even better reason to leave now and immediately tendered her resignation, but agreed to stay on as a consultant to transition in a new person. Public company CFO's have tremendous potential personal liability in these circumstances, so she wanted to get the heck out of dodge. Public CFO's have liability for the financial statements, for the commentary on those statements and for doing adequate fact checking (due diligence) before initiating and completing an acquisition. This moment is when I arrived as the new CFO.

My immediate recommendation was to close the newly acquired operation. John vetoed that idea. So, I brought in an industry consultant to see if the business could be salvaged. I also spoke to the two guys who had done the (supposed) due diligence to see what they suggested. One of the guys gave the new subsidiary some new business to try to help it. The other offered to take over running it to turn it around. We couldn't afford to pay the second guy what he wanted to take over the operation, so I asked the first of the three consultants to go spend two weeks at the operation and make recommendations.

The results of the review of BadCo by the industry consultant were beyond bad. First, there were serious human resources issues going on with multiple harassment claims against the division president who had been kept as part of the acquisition. The division president also was very poor on discipline, and the operation was in chaos (thus the huge losses). An immediate decision to terminate this legacy manager and have the consultant take over was made. The consultant implemented a disciplinary procedure that got the crew in line in a fair way, and the harassment stopped as soon as the cause of it was gone. It quickly became apparent though that no training of the staff had been done, and they didn't really know how to do their jobs. Many small companies just show new employees a desk and literally say get to work, and the new employees are too embarrassed to ask questions and admit that they don't know what they are doing. Also, some of the critical computer systems weren't working properly. We had BuyIt's in-house computer staff divert from the critical work for BuyIt to fix all the technical problems at BadCo, but fixing everything ended up taking six months and a ton of precious time of the IT staff. Also, the interruption to technical development of BuyIt's business was ultimately devastating. Acquisitions are huge distractions to the time and resources of the buyer. The buyer needs to be strong and stable to have a chance at success, and BuyIt was so far from being that that it wasn't even funny.

The final nail in the coffin proved to be that the major customers of BadCo had already given notice to BadCo prior to the acquisition that they were going to be terminating their contracts with it because of the turmoil within and poor performance, and revenue was going to drop precipitously. This critical detail was missed in the due diligence. Revenue plunged. My cost cutting had reduced the burn from $800,000 to $400,000 per month, but it was still a huge burn, and BuyIt was still burning $200,000 (down from its prior $400,000). Real progress had been made on the cost side, but it wasn't enough because a $600,000 cash loss a month is a tremendous challenge still. An 80% drop in revenue at BadCo ensued, and it became impossible to make payroll. A crash closure of the acquisition was ordered on a Thursday, with the business to close the next day on Friday. The consultant running it hired a U-Haul and a storage bin, loaded up all the equipment from BadCo, laid off the employees and walked away from the building. Six months later, BadCo's landlord tried to sue BuyIt for the balance of rent due on the lease, so more legal fees were generated and time was lost by me with court appearances, talking to lawyers and providing discovery. BadCo was the gift that kept on giving in a bad way.

The lesson here is that haste makes waste, the old expression goes, and waste it was, with millions of dollars lost and a lot of people out of work. Even worse, buying BadCo caused a tremendous distraction from the core business with serious damage to BuyIt's marketing, sales and IT development resources. Years later, BuyIt is still suffering from the wasted time and effort spent on an acquisition that was doomed to fail from the start by extremely poor due diligence. Buying revenue is a profoundly bad idea when executed poorly. If only companies would stay focused on the vision that led to their existence in the first place, the 80%+ first year failure rate would be substantially less. I hope that this book helps in some way.